Planning Function of Management

Planning means looking ahead and chalking out future courses of action to be followed. It is a preparatory step. It is a systematic activity which determines when, how and who is going to perform a specific job. Planning is a detailed programme regarding future courses of action. It is rightly said **"Well plan is half done"**. Therefore planning takes into consideration available & prospective human and physical resources of the organization so as to get effective co-ordination, contribution & perfect adjustment. It is the basic management function which includes formulation of one or more detailed plans to achieve optimum balance of needs or demands with the available resources.

According to Urwick, "Planning is a mental predisposition to do things in orderly way, to think before acting and to act in the light of facts rather than guesses". Planning is deciding best alternative among others to perform different managerial functions in order to achieve predetermined goals.

According to Koontz & O'Donell, "Planning is deciding in advance what to do, how to do and who is to do it. Planning bridges the gap between where we are to, where we want to go. It makes possible things to occur which would not otherwise occur".

Steps in Planning Function

Planning function of management involves following steps:-

1. **Establishment of objectives**
   a. Planning requires a systematic approach.
   b. Planning starts with the setting of goals and objectives to be achieved.
   c. Objectives provide a rationale for undertaking various activities as well as indicate direction of efforts.
   d. Moreover objectives focus the attention of managers on the end results to be achieved.
   e. As a matter of fact, objectives provide nucleus to the planning process. Therefore, objectives should be stated in a clear, precise and unambiguous language. Otherwise the activities undertaken are bound to be ineffective.
   f. As far as possible, objectives should be stated in quantitative terms. For example, Number of men working, wages given, units produced, etc. But such an objective cannot be stated in quantitative terms like performance of quality control manager, effectiveness of personnel manager.
   g. Such goals should be specified in qualitative terms.

h. Hence objectives should be practical, acceptable, workable and achievable.

2. **Establishment of Planning Premises**

a. Planning premises are the assumptions about the lively shape of events in future.

b. They serve as a basis of planning.

c. Establishment of planning premises is concerned with determining where one tends to deviate from the actual plans and causes of such deviations.

d. It is to find out what obstacles are there in the way of business during the course of operations.

e. Establishment of planning premises is concerned to take such steps that avoids these obstacles to a great extent.

f. Planning premises may be internal or external. Internal includes capital investment policy, management labour relations, philosophy of management, etc. Whereas external includes socio- economic, political and economical changes.

g. Internal premises are controllable whereas external are non- controllable.

3. **Choice of alternative course of action**

a. When forecast are available and premises are established, a number of alternative course of actions have to be considered.

b. For this purpose, each and every alternative will be evaluated by weighing its pros and cons in the light of resources available and requirements of the organization.

c. The merits, demerits as well as the consequences of each alternative must be examined before the choice is being made.

d. After objective and scientific evaluation, the best alternative is chosen.

e. The planners should take help of various quantitative techniques to judge the stability of an alternative.

4. **Formulation of derivative plans**

a. Derivative plans are the sub plans or secondary plans which help in the achievement of main plan.

b. Secondary plans will flow from the basic plan. These are meant to support and expediate the achievement of basic plans.

c. These detail plans include policies, procedures, rules, programmes, budgets, schedules, etc. For example, if profit maximization is the main aim of the enterprise, derivative plans will include sales maximization, production maximization, and cost minimization.

    d. Derivative plans indicate time schedule and sequence of accomplishing various tasks.

5.   **Securing Co-operation**

    a. After the plans have been determined, it is necessary rather advisable to take subordinates or those who have to implement these plans into confidence.

    b. The purposes behind taking them into confidence are :-

        i.   Subordinates may feel motivated since they are involved in decision making process.

        ii.   The organization may be able to get valuable suggestions and improvement in formulation as well as implementation of plans.

        iii.   Also the employees will be more interested in the execution of these plans.

6.   **Follow up/Appraisal of plans**

    a. After choosing a particular course of action, it is put into action.

    b. After the selected plan is implemented, it is important to appraise its effectiveness.

    c. This is done on the basis of feedback or information received from departments or persons concerned.

d. This enables the management to correct deviations or modify the plan.

e. This step establishes a link between planning and controlling function.

f. The follow up must go side by side the implementation of plans so that in the light of observations made, future plans can be made more realistic.

Characteristics of Planning

1. Planning is goal-oriented.

a. Planning is made to achieve desired objective of business.

b. The goals established should general acceptance otherwise individual efforts & energies will go misguided and misdirected.

c. Planning identifies the action that would lead to desired goals quickly & economically.

d. It provides sense of direction to various activities. E.g. Maruti Udhyog is trying to capture once again Indian Car Market by launching diesel models.

2. Planning is looking ahead.

a. Planning is done for future.

b. It requires peeping in future, analyzing it and

predicting it.

c. Thus planning is based on forecasting.

d. A plan is a synthesis of forecast.

e. It is a mental predisposition for things to happen in future.

3. Planning is an intellectual process.

a. Planning is a mental exercise involving creative thinking, sound judgement and imagination.

b. It is not a mere guesswork but a rotational thinking.

c. A manager can prepare sound plans only if he has sound judgement, foresight and imagination.

d. Planning is always based on goals, facts and considered estimates.

4. Planning involves choice & decision making.

a. Planning essentially involves choice among various alternatives.

b. Therefore, if there is only one possible course of action, there is no need planning because there is no choice.

c. Thus, decision making is an integral part of planning. A manager is surrounded by no. of alternatives. He has

d. to pick the best depending upon requirements & resources of the enterprises.

5. Planning is the primary function of management / Primacy of Planning.

a. Planning lays foundation for other functions of management.

b. It serves as a guide for organizing, staffing, directing and controlling.

c. All the functions of management are performed within the framework of plans laid out.

d. Therefore planning is the basic or fundamental function of management.

6. Planning is a Continuous Process.

a. Planning is a never ending function due to the dynamic business environment.

b. Plans are also prepared for specific period f time and at the end of that period, plans are subjected to revaluation and review in the light of new requirements and changing conditions.

c. Planning never comes into end till the enterprise exists issues, problems may keep cropping up and they have to be tackled by planning effectively.

7. Planning is all Pervasive.

    a. It is required at all <u>levels of management</u> and in all departments of enterprise.

    b. Of course, the scope of planning may differ from one level to another.

    c. The top level may be more concerned about planning the organization as a whole whereas the middle level may be more specific in departmental plans and the lower level plans implementation of the same.

8. Planning is designed for efficiency.

    a. Planning leads to accompishment of objectives at the minimum possible cost.

    b. It avoids wastage of resources and ensures adequate and optimum utilization of resources.

    c. A plan is worthless or useless if it does not value the cost incurred on it.

    d. Therefore planning must lead to saving of time, effort and money.

    e. Planning leads to proper utilization of men, money, materials, methods and machines.

9. Planning is Flexible.

    a. Planning is done for the future.

b. Since future is unpredictable, planning must provide enough room to cope with the changes in customer's demand, competition, govt. policies etc.

c. Under changed circumstances, the original plan of action must be revised and updated to male it more practical.

Advantages of Planning

1. Planning facilitates management by objectives.

   a. Planning begins with determination of objectives.

   b. It highlights the purposes for which various activities are to be undertaken.

   c. In fact, it makes objectives more clear and specific.

   d. Planning helps in focusing the attention of employees on the objectives or goals of enterprise.

   e. Without planning an organization has no guide.

   f. Planning compels manager to prepare a Blue-print of the courses of action to be followed for accomplishment of objectives.

   g. Therefore, planning brings order and rationality into the organization.

2. Planning minimizes uncertainties.

    a. Business is full of uncertainties.

    b. There are risks of various types due to uncertainties.

    c. Planning helps in reducing uncertainties of future as it involves anticipation of future events.

    d. Although future cannot be predicted with cent percent accuracy but planning helps management to anticipate future and prepare for risks by necessary provisions to meet unexpected turn of events.

    e. Therefore with the help of planning, uncertainties can be forecasted which helps in preparing standbys as a result, uncertainties are minimized to a great extent.

3. Planning facilitates co-ordination.

    a. Planning revolves around organizational goals.

    b. All activities are directed towards common goals.

    c. There is an integrated effort throughout the enterprise in various departments and groups.

    d. It avoids duplication of efforts. In other words, it leads to better co-ordination.

    e. It helps in finding out problems of work performance and aims at rectifying the same.

4. Planning improves employee's moral.

a. Planning creates an atmosphere of order and discipline in organization.

b. Employees know in advance what is expected of them and therefore conformity can be achieved easily.

c. This encourages employees to show their best and also earn reward for the same.

d. Planning creates a healthy attitude towards work environment which helps in boosting employees moral and efficiency.

5. Planning helps in achieving economies.

a. Effective planning secures economy since it leads to orderly allocation ofresources to various operations.

b. It also facilitates optimum utilization of resources which brings economy in operations.

c. It also avoids wastage of resources by selecting most appropriate use that will contribute to the objective of enterprise. For example, raw materials can be purchased in bulk and transportation cost can be minimized. At the same time it ensures regular supply for the production department, that is, overall efficiency.

6. Planning facilitates controlling.

a. Planning facilitates existence of certain planned goals and standard of performance.

b. It provides basis of controlling.

c. We cannot think of an effective system of controlling without existence of well thought out plans.

d. Planning provides pre-determined goals against which actual performance is compared.

e. In fact, planning and controlling are the two sides of a same coin. If planning is root, controlling is the fruit.

7. Planning provides competitive edge.

a. Planning provides competitive edge to the enterprise over the others which do not have effective planning. This is because of the fact that planning may involve changing in work methods, quality, quantity designs, extension of work, redefining of goals, etc.

b. With the help of forecasting not only the enterprise secures its future but at the same time it is able to estimate the future motives of it's competitor which helps in facing future challenges.

c. Therefore, planning leads to best utilization of possible resources, improves quality of production and thus the competitive strength of the enterprise is improved.

8. Planning encourages innovations.

    a. In the process of planning, managers have the opportunities of suggesting ways and means of improving performance.

Planning is basically a decision making function which involves creative thinking and imagination that ultimately leads to innovation of methods and operations for growth and prosperity of the enterprise.

Disadvantages of Planning

Internal Limitations

There are several limitations of planning. Some of them are inherit in the process of planning like rigidity and other arise due to shortcoming of the techniques of planning and in the planners themselves.

1. Rigidity

    a. Planning has tendency to make administration inflexible.

    b. Planning implies prior determination of policies, procedures and programmes and a strict adherence to them in all circumstances.

    c. There is no scope for individual freedom.

d. The development of employees is highly doubted because of which management might have faced lot of difficulties in future.

e. Planning therefore introduces inelasticity and discourages individual initiative and experimentation.

2. Misdirected Planning

a. Planning may be used to serve individual interests rather than the interest of the enterprise.

b. Attempts can be made to influence setting of objectives, formulation of plans and programmes to suit ones own requirement rather than that of whole organization.

c. Machinery of planning can never be freed of bias. Every planner has his own likes, dislikes, preferences, attitudes and interests which is reflected in planning.

3. Time consuming

a. Planning is a time consuming process because it involves collection of information, it's analysis and interpretation thereof. This entire process takes a lot of time specially where there are a number of alternatives available.

b. Therefore planning is not suitable during emergency or crisis when quick decisions are required.

4. Probability in planning

a. Planning is based on forecasts which are mere estimates about future.

b. These estimates may prove to be inexact due to the uncertainty of future.

c. Any change in the anticipated situation may render plans ineffective.

d. Plans do not always reflect real situations inspite of the sophisticated techniques of forecasting because future is unpredictable.

e. Thus, excessive reliance on plans may prove to be fatal.

5. False sense of security

a. Elaborate planning may create a false sense of security to the effect that everything is taken for granted.

b. Managers assume that as long as they work as per plans, it is satisfactory.

c. Therefore they fail to take up timely actions and an opportunity is lost.

d. Employees are more concerned about fulfillment of plan performance rather than any kind of change.

6. Expensive

    a. Collection, analysis and evaluation of different information, facts and alternatives involves a lot of expense in terms of time, effort and money

    b. According to Koontz and O'Donell, ' Expenses on planning should never exceed the estimated benefits from planning. '

External Limitations of Planning

1. Political Climate- Change of government from Congress to some other political party, etc.

2. Labour Union- Strikes, lockouts, agitations.

3. Technological changes- Modern techniques and equipments, computerization.

4. Policies of competitors- Eg. Policies of Coca Cola and Pepsi.

5. Natural Calamities- Earthquakes and floods.

6. Changes in demand and prices- Change in fashion, change in tastes, change in income level, demand falls, price falls, etc.

Organizing Function of Management

Organizing is the function of management which follows planning. It is a function in which the synchronization and combination of human, physical and financial resources takes place. All the three resources are important to get results. Therefore, organizational function helps in achievement of results which in fact is important for the functioning of a concern. According to *Chester Barnard*, "Organizing is a function by which the concern is able to define the role positions, the jobs related and the co- ordination between authority and responsibility. Hence, a manager always has to organize in order to get results.

A manager performs organizing function with the help of following steps:-

1. **Identification of activities** - All the activities which have to be performed in a concern have to be identified first. For example, preparation of accounts, making sales, record keeping, quality control, inventory control, etc. All these activities have to be grouped and classified into units.

2. **Departmentally organizing the activities** - In this step, the manager tries to combine and group similar and related activities into units or departments. This organization of dividing the whole concern into independent units and departments is called departmentation.

3. **Classifying the authority** - Once the departments are made, the manager likes to classify the powers and its extent to the managers. This activity of giving a rank in order to the managerial positions is called hierarchy. The top management is into formulation of policies, the middle level management into departmental supervision and lower level management into supervision of foremen. The clarification of authority help in bringing efficiency in the running of a concern. This helps in achieving efficiency in the running of a concern. This helps in avoiding wastage of time, money, effort, in avoidance of duplication or overlapping of efforts and this helps in bringing smoothness in a concern's working.

4. **Co-ordination between authority and responsibility** - Relationships are established among various groups to enable smooth interaction toward the achievment of the organizational goal. Each individual is made aware of his authority and he/she knows whom they have to take orders from and to whom they are accountable and to whom they have to report. A clear organizational structure is drawn and all the employees are made aware of it.

Importance of Organizing Function

Principles of Organizing

The organizing process can be done efficiently if the managers have certain guidelines so that they can take decisions and can act. To organize in an effective manner, the following principles of organization can be used by a manager.

1. Principle of Specialization

According to the principle, the whole work of a concern should be divided amongst the subordinates on the basis of qualifications, abilities and skills. It is through division of work specialization can be achieved which results in effective organization.

2. Principle of Functional Definition

According to this principle, all the functions in a concern should be completely and clearly defined to the managers and subordinates. This can be done by clearly defining the duties, responsibilities, authority and relationships of people towards each other. Clarifications in authority-responsibility relationships helps in achieving co- ordination and thereby organization can take place effectively. For example, the primary functions of production, marketing and finance and the authority responsibility relationships in these departments shouldbe clearly defined to every person attached to that department. Clarification in the authority-responsibility relationship helps in efficient organization.

3. Principles of Span of Control/Supervision

According to this principle, span of control is a span of supervision which depicts the number of employees that can be handled and controlled effectively by a single manager. According to this principle, a manager should be able to handle what number of employees under him should be decided. This decision can be taken by choosing either froma wide or narrow span. There are two types of span of control:-

   a. **Wide span of control-** It is one in which a manager can supervise and control effectively a large group of persons at one time. The features of this span are:-

      i.   Less overhead cost of supervision

      ii. Prompt response from the employees

      iii. Better communication

iv. Better supervision

v. Better co-ordination

vi. Suitable for repetitive jobs

According to this span, one manager can effectively and efficiently handle a large number of subordinates at one time.

b. **Narrow span of control-** According to this span, the work and authority is divided amongst many subordinates and a manager doesn't supervises and control a very big group of people under him. The manager according to a narrow span supervises a selected number of employees at one time. The features are:-

i. Work which requires tight control and supervision, for example, handicrafts, ivory work, etc. which requires craftsmanship, there narrow span is more helpful.

ii. Co-ordination is difficult to be achieved.

iii. Communication gaps can come.

iv. Messages can be distorted.

v. Specialization work can be achieved.

Factors influencing Span of Control

3.   **Managerial abilities-** In the concerns where managers are capable, qualified and experienced, wide span of control is always helpful.

4.   **Competence of subordinates-** Where the subordinates are capable and competent and their understanding levels are proper, the subordinates tend to very frequently visit the superiors for solving their problems. In such cases, the manager can handle large number of employees. Hence wide span is suitable.

5.   **Nature of work-** If the work is of repetitive nature, wide span of supervision is more helpful. On the other hand, if work requires mental skill or craftsmanship, tight control and supervision is required in which narrow span is more helpful.

6.   **Delegation of authority-** When the work is delegated to lower levels in an efficient and proper way, confusions are less and congeniality of the environment can be maintained. In such cases, wide span of control is suitable and the supervisors can manage and control large number of sub- ordinates at one time.

7.   **Degree of decentralization-** Decentralization is done in order to achieve specialization in which authority is shared by many people and managers at different levels. In such cases, a tall structure is helpful. There are certain concerns where

decentralization is done in very effective way which results in direct and personal communication between superiors and sub-ordinates and there the superiors can manage large number of subordinates very easily. In such cases, wide span again helps.

Principle of Scalar Chain

Scalar chain is a chain of command or authority which flows from top to bottom. With a chain of authority available, wastages of resources are minimized, communication is affected, overlapping of work is avoided and easy organization takes place. A scalar chain of command facilitates work flow in an organization which helps in achievement of effective results. As the authority flows from top to bottom, it clarifies the authority positions to managers at all level and that facilitates effective organization.

Principle of Unity of Command

It implies one subordinate-one superior relationship. Every subordinate is answerable and accountable to one boss at one time. This helps in avoiding communication gaps and feedback and response is prompt. Unity of command also helps in effective combination of resources, that is, physical, financial resources which helps in easy co- ordination and, therefore, effective organization.

Authority Flows from Top to Bottom

Managing Director

↓

Marketing Manager

↓

Sales/ Media Manager

↓

Salesmen

According to the above diagram, the Managing Director has got the highest level of authority. This authority is shared by the Marketing Manager who shares his authority with the Sales Manager. From this chain of hierarchy, the official chain of communication becomes clear which is helpful in achievement of results and which provides stability to a concern. This scalar chain of command always flow from top to bottom and it defines the authority positions of different managers at different levels.

Classification of Organizations

Organizations are basically clasified on the basis of relationships. There are two types of organizations formed on the basis of relationships in an organization

1. **Formal Organization** - This is one which refers to a structure of well defined jobs each bearing a measure of authority and responsibility. It is a conscious determination by which people accomplish goals by adhering to the norms laid down by the structure. This kind of organization is an arbitrary set up in which each person is responsible for his performance. Formal organization has a formal set up to achieve pre- determined goals.

2. **Informal Organization** - It refers to a network of personal and social relationships which spontaneously originates within the formal set up. Informal organizations develop relationships which are built on likes, dislikes, feelings and emotions. Therefore, the network of social groups based on friendships can be called as informal organizations. There is no conscious effort made to have informal organization. It emerges from the formal organization and it is not based on any rules and regulations as in case of formal organization.

Relationship between Formal and Informal Organizations

For a concerns working both formal and informal organization are important. Formal organization originates from the set organizational structure and informal organization originates from formal organization. For an efficient organization, both formal and informal organizations are required. They are the two phase of a same concern. Formal organization can work independently. But informal organization depends totally upon the formal organization. Formal and informal organization helps in bringing efficient working organization and smoothness in a concern. Within the formal organization, the members undertake the assigned duties in co- operation with each other. They interact and communicate amongst themselves. Therefore, both formal and informal organizations are important. When several people work together for achievement of organizational goals, social tie ups tends to built and therefore informal organization helps to secure co-operation by which goals can be achieved smooth. Therefore, we can say that informal organization emerges from formal organization.

Line Organization

Line organization is the most oldest and simplest method of administrative organization. According to this type of organization, the authority flows from top to bottom in a concern. The line of command is carried out from top to bottom. This is the reason for calling this organization as scalar organization which means scalar chain of command is a part and parcel of this type of administrative organization. In this type of organization, the line of command flows on an even basis without any gaps in communication and co- ordination taking place.

Features of Line Organization

1. It is the most simplest form of organization.
2. Line of authority flows from top to bottom.
3. Specialized and supportive services do not take place in these organization.
4. Unified control by the line officers can be maintained since they can independently take decisions in their areas and spheres.
5. This kind of organization always helps in bringing efficiency in communication and bringing stability to a concern.

Merits of Line Organization

1. **Simplest-** It is the most simple and oldest method of administration.

2. **Unity of Command-** In these organizations, superior-subordinate relationship is maintained and scalar chain of command flows from top to bottom.

3. **Better discipline-** The control is unified and concentrates on one person and therefore, he can independently make decisions of his own. Unified control ensures better discipline.

4. **Fixed responsibility-** In this type of organization, every line executive has got fixed authority, power and fixed responsibility attached to every authority.

5. **Flexibility-** There is a co-ordination between the top most authority and bottom line authority. Since the authority relationships are clear, line officials are independent and can flexibly take the decision. This flexibility gives satisfaction of line executives.

6. **Prompt decision-** Due to the factors of fixed responsibility and unity of command, the officials can take prompt decision.

Demerits of Line Organization

1. **Over reliance-** The line executive's decisions are implemented to the bottom. This results in over-relying on the line officials.

2. **Lack of specialization-** A line organization flows in a scalar chain from top to bottom and there is no scope for specialized functions. For example, expert advices whatever decisions are taken by line managers are implemented in the same way.

3. **Inadequate communication-** The policies and strategies which are framed by the top authority are carried out in the same way. This leaves no scope for communication from the other end. The complaints and suggestions of lower authority are not communicated back to the top authority. So there is one way communication.

4. **Lack of Co-ordination-** Whatever decisions are taken by the line officials, in certain situations wrong decisions, are carried down and implemented in the same way. Therefore, the degree of effective co- ordination is less.

5. **Authority leadership-** The line officials have tendency to misuse their authority positions. This leads to autocratic leadership and monopoly in the concern.

Line and Staff Organization

Line and staff organization is a modification of line organization and it is more complex than line organization. According to this administrative organization, specialized and supportive activities are attached to the line of command by appointing staff supervisors and staff specialists who are attached to the line authority. The power of command always remains with the line executives and staff supervisors guide, advice and council the line executives. Personal Secretary to the Managing Director is a staff official.

MANAGINGDIRECTOR

↓	↓	↓
Production Manager	Marketing Manager	Finance Manager
↓	↓	↓
Plant Supervisor	Market Supervisor	Chief Assisstant
↓	↓	↓
Foreman	Salesman	Accountant

Features of Line and Staff Organization

1. There are two types of staff :
    a. Staff Assistants- P.A. to Managing Director, Secretary to Marketing Manager.
    b. Staff Supervisor- Operation Control Manager, Quality Controller, PRO

2. Line and Staff Organization is a compromise of line organization. It is more complex than line concern.

3. Division of work and specialization takes place in line and staff organization.

4. The whole organization is divided into different functional areas to which staff specialists are attached.

5. Efficiency can be achieved through the features of specialization.

6. There are two lines of authority which flow at one time in a concern :

    a. Line Authority

    b. Staff Authority

7. Power of command remains with the line executive and staff serves only as counselors.

Merits of Line and Staff Organization

1. **Relief to line of executives-** In a line and staff organization, the advice and counseling which is provided to the line executives divides the work between the two. The line executive can concentrate on the execution of plans and they get relieved of dividing their attention to many areas.

2. **Expert advice-** The line and staff organization facilitates expert advice to the line executive at the time of need. The

planning and investigation which is related to different matters can be done by the staff specialist and line officers can concentrate on execution of plans.

3. **Benefit of Specialization-** Line and staff through division of whole concern into two types of authority divides the enterprise into parts and functional areas. This way every officer or official can concentrate in its own area.

4. **Better co-ordination-** Line and staff organization through specialization is able to provide better decision making and concentration remains in few hands. This feature helps in bringing co- ordination in work as every official is concentrating in their own area.

5. **Benefits of Research and Development-** Through the advice of specialized staff, the line executives, the line executives get time to execute plans by taking productive decisions which are helpful for a concern. This gives a wide scope to the line executive to bring innovations and go for research work in those areas. This is possible due to the presence of staff specialists.

6. **Training-** Due to the presence of staff specialists and their expert advice serves as ground for training to line officials. Line executives can give due concentration to their decision making. This in itself is a training ground for them.

7. **Balanced decisions-** The factor of specialization which is achieved by line staff helps in bringing co- ordination. This relationship automatically ends up the line official to take better and balanced decision.

8. **Unity of action-** Unity of action is a result of unified control. Control and its effectivity take place when co-ordination is present in the concern. In the line and staff authority all the officials have got independence to make decisions. This serves as effective control in the whole enterprise.

Demerits of Line and Staff Organization

1. **Lack of understanding-** In a line and staff organization, there are two authority flowing at one time. This results in the confusion between the two. As a result, the workers are not able to understand as to who is their commanding authority. Hence the problem of understanding can be a hurdle in effective running.

2. **Lack of sound advice-** The line official get used to the expertise advice of the staff. At times the staff specialist also provide wrong decisions which the line executive have to consider. This can affect the efficient running of the enterprise.

3. **Line and staff conflicts-** Line and staff are two authorities which are flowing at the same time. The factors of designations, status influence sentiments which are related to their relation, can pose a distress on the minds of the employees. This leads to minimizing of co- ordination which hampers a concern's working.

4. **Costly-** In line and staff concern, the concerns have to maintain the high remuneration of staff specialist. This proves to be costly for a concern with limited finance.

5. **Assumption of authority-** The power of concern is with the line official but the staff dislikes it as they are the one more in mental work.

6. **Staff steals the show-** In a line and staff concern, the higher returns are considered to be a product of staff advice and counseling. The line officials feel dissatisfied and a feeling of distress enters a concern. The satisfaction of line officials is very important for effective results.

Functional Organization

Functional organization has been divided to put the specialists in the top position throughout the enterprise. This is an organization in which we can define as a system in which functional department are created to deal with the problems of business at various levels. Functional authority remains confined to functional guidance to different departments. This helps in maintaining quality and uniformity of performance of different functions throughout the enterprise.

The concept of Functional organization was suggested by F.W. Taylor who recommended the appointment of specialists at important positions. For example, the functional head and Marketing Director directs the subordinates throughout the organization in his particular area. This means that subordinates receives orders from several specialists, managers working above them.

Features of Functional Organization

1. The entire organizational activities are divided into specific functions such as operations, finance, marketing and personal relations.

2. Complex form of administrative organization compared to the other two.

3. Three authorities exist- Line, staff and function.

4. Each functional area is put under the charge of functional specialists and he has got the authority to give all decisions

regarding the function whenever the function is performed throughout the enterprise.

5. Principle of unity of command does not apply to such organization as it is present in line organization.

Merits of Functional Organization

1. **Specialization-** Better division of labour takes place which results in specialization of function and it's consequent benefit.

2. **Effective Control-** Management control is simplified as the mental functions are separated from manual functions. Checks and balances keep the authority within certain limits. Specialists may be asked to judge the performance of various sections.

3. **Efficiency-** Greater efficiency is achieved because of every function performing a limited number of functions.

4. **Economy-** Specialization compiled with standardization facilitates maximum production and economical costs.

5. **Expansion-** Expert knowledge of functional manager facilitates better control and supervision.

Demerits of Functional Organization

1. **Confusion-** The functional system is quite complicated to put into operation, especially when it is carried out at low levels. Therefore, co- ordination becomes difficult.

2. **Lack of Co- ordination-** Disciplinary control becomes weak as a worker is commanded not by one person but a large number of people. Thus, there is no unity of command.

3. **Difficulty in fixing responsibility-** Because of multiple authority, it is difficult to fix responsibility.

4. **Conflicts-** There may be conflicts among the supervisory staff of equal ranks. They may not agree on certain issues.

Costly- Maintainance of specialist's staff of the highest order is expensive for a concern.

Delegation of Authority - Meaning, Importance and its Principles

A manager alone cannot perform all the tasks assigned to him. In order to meet the targets, the manager should delegate authority. Delegation of Authority means division of authority and powers downwards to the subordinate. Delegation is about entrusting someone else to do parts of your job. Delegation of authority can be defined as subdivision and sub-allocation of powers to the subordinates in order to achieve effective results.

Elements of Delegation

1. **Authority** - in context of a business organization, authority can be defined as the power and right of a person to use and allocate the resources efficiently, to take decisions and to give orders so as to achieve the organizational objectives. Authority must be well- defined. All people who have the authority should know what is the scope of their authority is and they shouldn't misutilize it. Authority is the right to give commands, orders and get the things done. The top level management has greatest authority. Authority always flows from top to bottom. It explains how a superior gets work done from his subordinate by clearly explaining what is expected of him and how he should go about it. Authority should be accompanied with an equal amount of responsibility. Delegating the authority to someone else doesn't imply escaping from accountability. Accountability still rest with the person having the utmost authority.

For achieving delegation, a manager has to work in a system and has to perform following steps : -

1. Assignment of tasks and duties

2. Granting of authority

3. Creating responsibility and accountability

Delegation of authority is the base of superior-subordinate relationship, it involves following steps:-

1. **Assignment of Duties** - The delegator first tries to define the task and duties to the subordinate. He also has to define the result expected from the subordinates. Clarity of duty as well as result expected has to be the first step in delegation.

2. **Granting of authority** - Subdivision of authority takes place when a superior divides and shares his authority with the subordinate. It is for this reason, every subordinate should be given enough independence to carry the task given to him by his superiors. The managers at all levels delegate authority and power which is attached to their job positions. The subdivision of powers is very important to get effective results.

3. **Creating Responsibility and Accountability** - The delegation process does not end once powers are granted to the subordinates. They at the same time have to be obligatory towards the duties assigned to them. Responsibility is said to be the factor or obligation of an individual to carry out his duties in best of his ability as per

the directions of superior. Responsibility is very important. Therefore, it is that which gives effectiveness to authority. At the same time, responsibility is absolute and cannot be shifted. Accountability, on the others hand, is the obligation of the individual to carry out his duties as per the standards of performance. Therefore, it is said that authority is delegated, responsibility is created and accountability is imposed. Accountability arises out of responsibility and responsibility arises out of authority. Therefore, it becomes important that with every authority position an equal and opposite responsibility should be attached.

Therefore every manager,i.e.,the delegator has to follow a system to finish up the delegation process. Equally important is the delegatee's role which means his responsibility and accountability is attached with the authority over to here.

Relationship between Authority and Responsibility

Authority is the legal right of person or superior to command his subordinates while accountability is the obligation of individual to carry out his duties as per standards of performance Authority flows from the superiors to subordinates,in which orders and instructions are given to subordinates to complete the task. It is only through authority, a manager exercises control. In a way through exercising the control the superior is demanding accountability from subordinates. If the marketing manager directs the sales supervisor for 50 units of sale to be undertaken in a month. If the above standards are not accomplished, it is the marketing manager who will be accountable to the chief executive officer. Therefore, we can say that authority flows from top to bottom and responsibility flows from bottom to top. Accountability is a result of responsibility and responsibility is result of authority. Therefore, for every authority an equal accountability is attached.

Differences between Authority and Responsibility

Authority	Responsibility
It is the legal right of a person or a superior to command his subordinates.	It is the obligation of subordinate to perform the work assigned to him.
Authority is attached to the position of a superior in concern.	Responsibility arises out of superior-subordinate relationship in which

	subordinate agrees to carry out duty given to him.
Authority can be delegated by a superior to a subordinate	Responsibility cannot be shifted and is absolute
It flows from top to bottom.	It flows from bottom to top.

Importance of Delegation

Delegation of authority is a process in which the authority and powers are divided and shared amongst the subordinates. When the work of a manager gets beyond his capacity, there should be some system of sharing the work. This is how delegation of authority becomes an important tool in organization function. Through delegation, a manager, in fact, is multiplying himself by dividing/multiplying his work with the subordinates. The importance of delegation can be justified by -

1. Through delegation, a manager is able to divide the work and allocate it to the subordinates. This helps in reducing his

work load so that he can work on important areas such as - planning, business analysis etc.

2. With the reduction of load on superior, he can concentrate his energy on important and critical issues of concern. This way he is able to bring effectiveness in his work as well in the work unit. This effectivity helps a manager to prove his ability and skills in the best manner.

3. Delegation of authority is the ground on which the superior-subordinate relationship stands. An organization functions as the authority flows from top level to bottom. This in fact shows that through delegation, the superior-subordinate relationship become meaningful. The flow of authority is from top to bottom which is a way of achieving results.

4. Delegation of authority in a way gives enough room and space to the subordinates to flourish their abilities and skill. Through delegating powers, the subordinates get a feeling of importance. They get motivated to work and this motivation provides appropriate results to a concern. Job satisfaction is an important criterion to bring stability and soundness in the relationship between superior and subordinates. Delegation also helps in breaking the monotony of the subordinates so that they can be more creative and efficient. Delegation of

authority is not only helpful to the subordinates but it also helps the managers to develop their talents and skills. Since the manager get enough time through delegation to concentrate on important issues, their decision-making gets strong and in a way they can flourish the talents which are required in a manager. Through granting powers and getting the work done, helps the manager to attain communication skills, supervision and guidance, effective motivation and the leadership traits are flourished. Therefore it is only through delegation, a manager can be tested on his traits.

5. Delegation of authority is help to both superior and subordinates. This, in a way, gives stability to a concern's working. With effective results, a concern can think of creating more departments and divisions flow working. This will require creation of more managers which can be fulfilled by shifting the experienced, skilled managers to these positions. This helps in both virtual as well as horizontal growth which is very important for a concern's stability.

Therefore, from the above points, we can justify that delegation is not just a process but it is a way by which manager multiples himself and is able to bring stability, ability and soundness to a concern.

Principles of Delegation

There are a few guidelines in form of principles which can be a help to the manager to process of delegation. The **principles of delegation** are as follows: -

1. **Principle of result excepted-** suggests that every manager before delegating the powers to the subordinate should be able to clearly define the goals as well as results expected from them. The goals and targets should be completely and clearly defined and the standards of performance should also be notified clearly. For example, a marketing manager explains the salesmen regarding the units of sale to take place in a particular day, say ten units a day have to be the target sales. While a marketing manger provides these guidelines of sales, mentioning the target sales is very important so that the salesman can perform his duty efficiently with a clear set of mind.

2. **Principle of Parity of Authority and Responsibility-** According to this principle, the manager should keep a balance between authority and responsibility. Both of them should go hand in hand.

According to this principle, if a subordinate is given a responsibility to perform a task, then at the same time he should be given enough independence and power to carry out that task effectively. This principle also does not provide excessive authority to the subordinate which at times can be misused by him. The authority should be given in such a way which matches the task given to him. Therefore, there should be no degree of disparity between the two.

3. **Principle of absolute responsibility-** This says that the authority can be delegated but responsibility cannot be delegated by managers to his subordinates which means responsibility is fixed. The manager at every level, no matter what is his authority, is always responsible to his superior for carrying out his task by delegating the powers. It does not means that he can escape from his responsibility. He will always remain responsible till the completion of task. Every superior is responsible for the acts of their subordinates and are accountable to their superior therefore the superiors cannot pass the blame to the subordinates even if he has delegated certain powers to subordinates example if the production manager has been given a work and the machine breaks down. If repairmen is not able to get repair work

done, production manager will be responsible to CEO if their production is not completed.

4. **Principle of Authority level-** This principle suggests that a manager should exercise his authority within the jurisdiction / framework given. The manager should be forced to consult their superiors with those matters of which the authority is not given that means before a manager takes any important decision, he should make sure that he has the authority to do that on the other hand, subordinate should also not frequently go with regards to their complaints as well as suggestions to their superior if they are not asked to do. This principle emphasizes on the degree of authority and the level upto which it has to be maintained.

Centralization and Decentralization

Centralization is said to be a process where the concentration of decision making is in a few hands. All the important decision and actions at the lower level, all subjects and actions at the lower level are subject to the approval of top management. According to Allen, "Centralization" is the systematic and consistent reservation of authority at central points in the organization. The implication of centralization can be :-

1. Reservation of decision making power at top level.

2. Reservation of operating authority with the middle level managers.

3. Reservation of operation at lower level at the directions of the top level.

Under centralization, the important and key decisions are taken by the top management and the other levels are into implementations as per the directions of top level. For example, in a business concern, the father & son being the owners decide about the important matters and all the rest of functions

like product, finance, marketing, personnel, are carried out by the department heads and they have to act as per instruction and orders of the two people. Therefore in this case, decision making power remain in the hands of father & son.

On the other hand, **Decentralization** is a systematic delegation of authority at all levels of management and in all of the organization. In a decentralization concern, authority in retained by the top management for taking major decisions and framing policies concerning the whole concern. Rest of the authority may be delegated to the middle level and lower level of management.

The degree of **centralization and decentralization** will depend upon the amount of authority delegated to the lowest level.

According to Allen, "Decentralization refers to the systematic effort to delegate to the lowest level of authority except that which can be controlled and exercised at central points.

Decentralization is not the same as delegation. In fact, decentralization is all extension of delegation. Decentralization pattern is wider is scope and the authorities are diffused to the lowest most level of management. Delegation of authority is a complete process and takes place from one person to another. While decentralization is complete only when fullest possible delegation has taken place. For example, the general manager of a company is responsible for receiving the leave application for the whole of the concern. The general manager delegates this work to the personnel manager who is now responsible for receiving the leave applicants. In this situation delegation of authority has taken place. On the other hand, on the request of the personnel manager, if the general manager delegates this power to all the departmental heads at all level, in this situation decentralization has taken place. There is a saying that "Everything that increasing the role of subordinates is decentralization and that decreases the role is centralization". Decentralization is wider in scope and the subordinate's responsibility increase in this case. On the other hand, in delegation the managers remain answerable even for the acts of subordinates to their superiors.

Implications of Decentralization

1. There is less burden on the Chief Executive as in the case of centralization.

2. In decentralization, the subordinates get a chance to decide and act independently which develops skills and capabilities. This way the organization is able to process reserve of talents in it.

3. In decentralization, diversification and horizontal can be easily implanted.

4. In decentralization, concern diversification of activities can place effectively since there is more scope for creating new departments. Therefore, diversification growth is of a degree.

5. In decentralization structure, operations can be coordinated at divisional level which is not possible in the centralization set up.

6. In the case of decentralization structure, there is greater motivation and morale of the employees since they get more independence to act and decide.

7. In a decentralization structure, co-ordination to some extent is difficult to maintain as there are lot many department divisions and authority is delegated to maximum possible extent, i.e., to the bottom most level delegation reaches. Centralization and decentralization are the categories by which the pattern of authority relationships became clear. The degree of centralization and de-centralization can be affected by many factors like nature of operation, volume of profits, number of departments, size of a concern, etc. The larger the size of a concern, a decentralization set up is suitable in it.

Delegation and Decentralization

Basis	Delegation	Decentralization
Meaning	Managers delegate some of their function and authority to their subordinates.	Right to take decisions is shared by top management and other level of management.
Scope	Scope of delegation is limited as superior	Scope is wide as the decision making is shared

	delegates the powers to the subordinates on individual bases.	by the subordinates also.
Responsibility	Responsibility remains of the managers and cannot be delegated	Responsibility is also delegated to subordinates.
Freedom of Work	Freedom is not given to the subordinates as they have to work as per the instructions of their superiors.	Freedom to work can be maintained by subordinates as they are free to take decision and to implement it.
Nature	It is a routine function	It is an important decision of an enterprise.
Need on purpose	Delegation is important in all concerns whether big or small. No enterprises can work	Decentralization becomes more important in large concerns and it depends upon the decision made by the enterprise, it is not

	without delegation.	compulsory.
Grant of Authority	The authority is granted by one individual to another.	It is a systematic act which takes place at all levels and at all functions in a concern.
Grant of Responsibility	Responsibility cannot be delegated	Authority with responsibility is delegated to subordinates.
Degree	Degree of delegation varies from concern to concern and department to department.	Decentralization is total by nature. It spreads throughout the organization i.e. at all levels and all functions
Process	Delegation is a process which explains superior subordinates relationship	It is an outcome which explains relationship between top management and all other departments.
Essentiality	Delegation is	Decentralization is a

	essential of all kinds of concerns	decisions function by nature.
Significance	Delegation is essential for creating the organization	Decentralization is an optional policy at the discretion of top management.
Withdrawal	Delegated authority can be taken back.	It is considered as a general policy of top management and is applicable to all departments.
Freedom of Action	Very little freedom to the subordinates	Considerable freedom

Decentralization can be called as extension of delegation. When delegation of authority is done to the fullest possible extent, it gives use to decentralization.

Staffing Function of Management

The managerial function of staffing involves manning the organization structure through proper and effective selection, appraisal and development of the personnels to fill the roles assigned to the employers/workforce.

According to Theo Haimann, "Staffing pertains to recruitment, selection, development and compensation of subordinates."

Nature of Staffing Function

Staffing is an important managerial function- Staffing function is the most important mangerial act along with planning, organizing, directing and controlling. The operations of these four functions depend upon the manpower which is available through staffing function.

Staffing is a pervasive activity- As staffing function is carried out by all mangers and in all types of concerns where business activities are carried out.

Staffing is a continuous activity- This is because staffing function continues throughout the life of an organization due to the transfers and promotions that take place.

The basis of staffing function is efficient management of personnels- Human resources can be efficiently managed by a system or proper procedure, that is, recruitment, selection, placement, training and development, providing remuneration, etc.

Staffing helps in placing right men at the right job. It can be done effectively through proper recruitment procedures and then finally selecting the most suitable candidate as per the job requirements.

Staffing is performed by all managers depending upon the nature of business, size of the company, qualifications and skills of managers,etc. In small companies, the top management generally performs this function. In medium and small scale enterprise, it is performed especially by the personnel department of that concern.

Staffing Process - Steps involved in Staffing

1. **Manpower requirements-** The very first step in staffing is to plan the manpower inventory required by a concern in order to match them with the job requirements and demands. Therefore, it involves forecasting and determining the future manpower needs of the concern.

2. **Recruitment-** Once the requirements are notified, the concern invites and solicits applications according to the invitations made to the desirable candidates.

3. **Selection-** This is the screening step of staffing in which the solicited applications are screened out and suitable candidates are appointed as per the requirements.

4. **Orientation and Placement-** Once screening takes place,

the appointed candidates are made familiar to the work units and work environment through the orientation programmes. placement takes place by putting right man on the right job.

5. **Training and Development-** Training is a part of incentives given to the workers in order to develop and grow them within the concern. Training is generally given according to the nature of activities and scope of expansion in it. Along with it, the workers are developed by providing them extra benefits of indepth knowledge of their functional areas. Development also includes giving them key and important jobsas a test or examination in order to analyse their performances.

6. **Remuneration-** It is a kind of compensation provided monetarily to the employees for their work performances. This is given according to the nature of job- skilled or unskilled, physical or mental, etc. Remuneration forms an important monetary incentive for the employees.

7. **Performance Evaluation-** In order to keep a track or record of the behaviour, attitudes as well as opinions of the workers towards their jobs. For this regular assessment is done to evaluate and supervise different work units in a concern. It is basically concerning to know the development cycle and

growth patterns of the employeesin a concern.

8. **Promotion and transfer-** Promotion is said to be a non-monetary incentive in which the worker is shifted from a higher job demanding bigger responsibilities as well as shifting the workers and transferring them to different work units and branches of the same organization.

Manpower Planning

Manpower Planning which is also called as Human Resource Planning consists of putting right number of people, right kind of people at the right place, right time, doing the right things for which they are suited for the achievement of goals of the organization. Human Resource Planning has got an important place in the arena of industrialization. Human Resource Planning has to be a systems approach and is carried out in a set procedure. The procedure is as follows:

1. Analysing the current manpower inventory
2. Making future manpower forecasts
3. Developing employment programmes
4. Design training programmes

Steps in Manpower Planning

1. **Analysing the current manpower inventory-** Before a manager makes forecast of future manpower, the current manpower status has to be analysed. For this the following things have to be noted-

   - Type of organization
   - Number of departments
   - Number and quantity of such departments
   - Employees in these work units

   Once these factors are registered by a manager, he goes for the future forecasting.

2. **Making future manpower forecasts-** Once the factors affecting the future manpower forecasts are known, planning can be done for the future manpower requirements in several work units.

   The Manpower forecasting techniques commonly employed by the organizations are as follows:

   i. **Expert Forecasts:** This includes informal decisions, formal expert surveys and Delphi technique.

   ii. **Trend Analysis:** Manpower needs can be projected through extrapolation (projecting past trends), indexation (using base year as basis), and statistical analysis (central tendency measure).

iii. **Work Load Analysis:** It is dependent upon the nature of work load in a department, in a branch or in a division.

iv. **Work Force Analysis:** Whenever production and time period has to be analysed, due allowances have to be made for getting net manpower requirements.

v. **Other methods:** Several Mathematical models, with the aid of computers are used to forecast manpower needs, like budget and planning analysis, regression, new venture analysis.

3. **Developing employment programmes-** Once the current inventory is compared with future forecasts, the employment programmes can be framed and developed accordingly, which will include recruitment, selection procedures and placement plans.

4. **Design training programmes-** These will be based upon extent of diversification, expansion plans, development programmes,etc. Training programmes depend upon the extent of improvement in technology and advancement to take place. It is also done to improve upon the skills, capabilities, knowledge of the workers.

Importance of Manpower Planning

1. **Key to managerial functions-** The four managerial functions, i.e., planning, organizing, directing and controlling are based upon the manpower. Human resources help in the implementation of all these managerial activities. Therefore, staffing becomes a key to all managerial functions.

2. **Efficient utilization-** Efficient management of personnels becomes an important function in the industrialization world of today. Seting of large scale enterprises require management of large scale manpower. It can be effectively done through staffing function.

3. **Motivation-** Staffing function not only includes putting right men on right job, but it also comprises of motivational programmes, i.e., incentive plans to be framed for further participation and employment of employees in a concern. Therefore, all types of incentive plans becomes an integral part of staffing function.

4. **Better human relations-** A concern can stabilize itself if human relations develop and are strong. Human relations become strong trough effective control, clear communication, effective supervision and leadership in a

concern. Staffing function also looks after training and development of the work force which leads to co-operation and better human relations.

5. **Higher productivity-** Productivity level increases when resources are utilized in best possible manner. higher productivity is a result of minimum wastage of time, money, efforts and energies. This is possible through the staffing and it's related activities (Performance appraisal, training and development, remuneration)

Need of Manpower Planning

Manpower Planning is a two-phased process because manpower planning not only analyses the current human resources but also makes manpower forecasts and thereby draw employment programmes. Manpower Planning is advantageous to firm in following manner:

1. Shortages and surpluses can be identified so that quick action can be taken wherever required.
2. All the recruitment and selection programmes are based on manpower planning.
3. It also helps to reduce the labour cost as excess staff can be identified and thereby overstaffing can be avoided.

4. It also helps to identify the available talents in a concern and accordingly training programmes can be chalked out to develop those talents.

5. It helps in growth and diversification of business. Through manpower planning, human resources can be readily available and they can be utilized in best manner.

6. It helps the organization to realize the importance of manpower management which ultimately helps in the stability of a concern.

Obstacles in Manpower Planning

Following are the main obstacles that organizations face in the process of manpower planning:

1. **Under Utilization of Manpower:** The biggest obstacle in case of manpower planning is the fact that the industries in general are not making optimum use of their manpower and once manpower planning begins, it encounters heavy odds in stepping up the utilization.

2. **Degree of Absenteeism:** Absenteeism is quite high and has been increasing since last few years.

3. **Lack of Education and Skilled Labour:** The extent of illetracy and the slow pace of development of the skilled

categories account for low productivity in employees. Low productivity has implications for manpower planning.

4. **Manpower Control and Review:**

   a. Any increase in manpower is considered at the top level of management

   b. On the basis of manpower plans, personnel budgets are prepared. These act as control mechanisms to keep the manpower under certain broadly defined limits.

   c. The productivity of any organization is usually calculated using the formula:

   Productivity = Output / Input

   . But a rough index of employee productivity is calculated as follows:

   Employee Productivity = Total Production / Total no. of employees

   d. Exit Interviews, the rate of turnover and rate of absenteesim are source of vital information on the satisfaction level of manpower. For conservation of Human Resources and better utilization of men studying these condition, manpower control would have to take into account the data to make meaningful analysis.

e. Extent of Overtime: The amount of overtime paid may be due to real shortage of men, ineffective management or improper utilization of manpower. Manpower control would require a careful study of overtime statistics.

Few Organizations do not have sufficient records and information on manpower. Several of those who have them do not have a proper retrieval system. There are complications in resolving the issues in design, definition and creation of computerized personnel information system for effective manpower planning and utilization. Even the existing technologies in this respect is not optimally used. This is a strategic disadvantage.

Types of Recruitment

Recruitment is of 2 types

1. **Internal Recruitment** - is a recruitment which takes place within the concern or organization. Internal sources of recruitment are readily available to an organization. Internal sources are primarily three - Transfers, promotions and Re-employment of ex-employees. Re-employment of ex-

employees is one of the internal sources of recruitment in which employees can be invited and appointed to fill vacancies in the concern. There are situations when ex-employees provide unsolicited applications also.

Internal recruitment may lead to increase in employee's productivity as their motivation level increases. It also saves time, money and efforts. But a drawback of internal recruitment is that it refrains the organization from new blood. Also, not all the manpower requirements can be met through internal recruitment. Hiring from outside has to be done.

Internal sources are primarily 3

a. **Transfers**

b. **Promotions (through Internal Job Postings)** and

c. **Re-employment of ex-employees** - Re-employment of ex-employees is one of the internal sources of recruitment in which employees can be invited and appointed to fill vacancies in the concern. There are situations when ex-employees provide unsolicited applications also.

2. **External Recruitment** - External sources of recruitment have to be solicited from outside the organization. External

sources are external to a concern. But it involves lot of time and money. The external sources of recruitment include - Employment at factory gate, advertisements, employment exchanges, employment agencies, educational institutes, labour contractors, recommendations etc.

a. **Employment at Factory Level** - This a source of external recruitment in which the applications for vacancies are presented on bulletin boards outside the Factory or at the Gate. This kind of recruitment is applicable generally where factory workers are to be appointed. There are people who keep on soliciting jobs from one place to another. These applicants are called as unsolicited applicants. These types of workers apply on their own for their job. For this kind of recruitment workers have a tendency to shift from one factory to another and therefore they are called as "badli" workers.

b. **Advertisement** - It is an external source which has got an important place in recruitment procedure. The biggest advantage of advertisement is that it covers a wide area of market and scattered applicants can get information from advertisements. Medium used is Newspapers and Television.

c. **Employment Exchanges** - There are certain Employment exchanges which are run by government. Most of the government undertakings and concerns employ people through such exchanges. Now-a-days recruitment in government agencies has become compulsory through employment exchange.

d. **Employment Agencies** - There are certain professional organizations which look towards recruitment and employment of people, i.e. these private agencies run by private individuals supply required manpower to needy concerns.

e. **Educational Institutions** - There are certain professional Institutions which serves as an external source for recruiting fresh graduates from these institutes. This kind of recruitment done through such educational institutions, is called as Campus Recruitment. They have special recruitment cells which helps in providing jobs to fresh candidates.

f. **Recommendations** - There are certain people who have experience in a particular area. They enjoy goodwill and a stand in the company. There are certain vacancies which are filled by recommendations of such people. The biggest drawback of this source is that the company has to rely totally on such people which can later on prove to be inefficient.

g. **Labour Contractors** - These are the specialist people who supply manpower to the Factory or Manufacturing plants. Through these contractors, workers are appointed on contract basis, i.e. for a particular time period. Under conditions when these contractors leave the organization, such people who are appointed have to also leave the concern.

Employee Selection Process

Employee Selection is the process of putting right men on right job. It is a procedure of matching organizational requirements with the skills and qualifications of people. Effective selection can be done only when there is effective matching. By selecting best candidate for the required job, the organization will get quality performance of employees. Moreover, organization will face less of absenteeism and employee turnover problems. By selecting right candidate for the required job, organization will also save time and money. Proper screening of candidates takes place during selection procedure. All the potential candidates who apply for the given job are tested.

But selection must be differentiated from recruitment, though these are two phases of employment process. Recruitment is considered to be a positive process as it motivates more of candidates to apply for the job. It creates a pool of applicants. It is just sourcing of data. While selection is a negative process as the inappropriate candidates are rejected here. Recruitment precedes selection in staffing process. Selection involves choosing the best candidate with best abilities, skills and knowledge for the required job.

The **Employee selection Process** takes place in following order-

1. **Preliminary Interviews-** It is used to eliminate those candidates who do not meet the minimum eligiblity criteria laid down by the organization. The skills, academic and family background, competencies and interests of the candidate are examined during preliminary interview. Preliminary interviews are less formalized and planned than the final interviews. The candidates are given a brief up about the company and the job profile; and it is also examined how much the candidate knows about the company. Preliminary interviews are also called screening interviews.

2. **Application blanks-** The candidates who clear the preliminary interview are required to fill application blank. It contains data record of the candidates such as details about age, qualifications, reason for leaving previous job, experience, etc.

3. **Written Tests-** Various written tests conducted during selection procedure are aptitude test, intelligence test, reasoning test, personality test, etc. These tests are used to objectively assess the potential candidate. They should not be biased.

4. **Employment Interviews-** It is a one to one interaction between the interviewer and the potential candidate. It is used to find whether the candidate is best suited for the required job or not. But such interviews consume time and money both. Moreover the competencies of the candidate cannot be judged. Such interviews may be biased at times. Such interviews should be conducted properly. No distractions should be there in room. There should be an honest communication between candidate and interviewer.

5. **Medical examination-** Medical tests are conducted to ensure physical fitness of the potential employee. It will decrease chances of employee absenteeism.

6. **Appointment Letter-** A reference check is made about the candidate selected and then finally he is appointed by giving a formal appointment letter.

Difference between Recruitment and Selection

Basis	Recruitment	Selection
Meaning	It is an activity of establishing contact between employers and applicants.	It is a process of picking up more competent and suitable employees.
Objective	It encourages large number of Candidates for a job.	It attempts at rejecting unsuitable candidates.
Process	It is a simple process.	It is a complicated process.
Hurdles	The candidates have not to cross over many hurdles.	Many hurdles have to be crossed.
Approach	It is a positive approach.	It is a negative approach.

Sequence	It proceeds selection.	It follows recruitment.
Economy	It is an economical method.	It is an expensive method.
Time Consuming	Less time is required.	More time is required.

Orientation and Placement

Once the candidates are selected for the required job, they have to be fitted as per the qualifications. Placement is said to be the process of fitting the selected person at the right job or place, i.e. fitting square pegs in square holes and round pegs in round holes. Once he is fitted into the job, he is given the activities he has to perform and also told about his duties. The freshly appointed candidates are then given orientation in order to familiarize and introduce the company to him. Generally the information given during the orientation programme includes-

- Employee's layout
- Type of organizational structure
- Departmental goals
- Organizational layout
- General rules and regulations

- Standing Orders
- Grievance system or procedure

In short, during Orientation employees are made aware about the mission and vision of the organization, the nature of operation of the organization, policies and programmes of the organization.

The main aim of conducting Orientation is to build up confidence, morale and trust of the employee in the new organization, so that he becomes a productive and an efficient employee of the organization and contributes to the organizational success.

The nature of Orientation program varies with the organizational size, i.e., smaller the organization the more informal is the Orientation and larger the organization more formalized is the Orientation programme.

Proper Placement of employees will lower the chances of employee's absenteeism. The employees will be more satisfied and contended with their work.

Training of Employees - Need and Importance of Training

Training of employees takes place after orientation takes place. Training is the process of enhancing the skills, capabilities and knowledge of employees for doing a particular job. Training process moulds the thinking of employees and leads to quality performance of employees. It is continuous and never ending in nature.

Importance of Training

Training is crucial for organizational development and success. It is fruitful to both employers and employees of an organization. An employee will become more efficient and productive if he is trained well.

Training is given on four basic grounds:

1. New candidates who join an organization are given training. This training familiarize them with the organizational mission, vision, rules and regulations and the working conditions.

2. The existing employees are trained to refresh and enhance their knowledge.

3. If any updations and amendments take place in technology, training is given to cope up with those changes. For instance, purchasing a new equipment, changes in technique of production, computer implantment. The employees are trained about use of new equipments and work methods.

4. When promotion and career growth becomes important. Training is given so that employees are prepared to share the responsibilities of the higher level job.

The benefits of training can be summed up as:

1. **Improves morale of employees-** Training helps the employee to get job security and job satisfaction. The more satisfied the employee is and the greater is his morale, the more he will contribute to organizational success and the lesser will be employee absenteeism and turnover.

2. **Less supervision-** A well trained employee will be well acquainted with the job and will need less of supervision. Thus, there will be less wastage of time and efforts.

3. **Fewer accidents-** Errors are likely to occur if the employees lack knowledge and skills required for doing a particular job. The more trained an employee is, the less are the chances of committing accidents in job and the more proficient the employee becomes.

4. **Chances of promotion-** Employees acquire skills and efficiency during training. They become more eligible for promotion. They become an asset for the organization.

5. **Increased productivity-** Training improves efficiency and productivity of employees. Well trained employees show

both quantity and quality performance. There is less wastage of time, money and resources if employees are properly trained.

Ways/Methods of Training

Training is generally imparted in two ways:

1. **On the job training-** On the job training methods are those which are given to the employees within the everyday working of a concern. It is a simple and cost-effective training method. The inproficient as well as semi- proficient employees can be well trained by using such training method. The employees are trained in actual working scenario. The motto of such training is "learning by doing." Instances of such on-job training methods are job-rotation, coaching, temporary promotions, etc.

2. **Off the job training-** Off the job training methods are those in which training is provided away from the actual working condition. It is generally used in case of new employees. Instances of off the job training methods are workshops, seminars, conferences, etc. Such method is costly and is effective if and only if large number of employees have to be trained within a short time period. Off the job training is also called as vestibule training,i.e., the employees are

trained in a separate area(may be a hall, entrance, reception area,etc. known as a vestibule) where the actual working conditions are duplicated.

Employee Remuneration

Employee Remuneration refers to the reward or compensation given to the employees for their work performances. Remuneration provides basic attraction to a employee to perform job efficiently and effectively. Remuneration leads to employee motivation. Salaries constitutes an important source of income for employees and determine their standard of living. Salaries effect the employees productivity and work performance. Thus the amount and method of remuneration are very important for both management and employees.

There are mainly two types of Employee Remuneration

1. **Time Rate Method**
2. **Piece Rate Method**

These methods of employee remuneration are explained below in detail

Methods of Employee Remuneration

1. **Time Rate Method:** Under time rate system, remuneration is directly linked with the time spent or devoted by an employee on the job. The employees are paid a fixed pre-decided amount hourly, daily, weekly or monthly irrespective of their output. It is a very simple method of remuneration. It leads to minimum wastage of resources and lesser chances of accidents. Time Rate method leads to quality output and this method is very beneficial to new employees as they can learn their work without any reduction in their salaries. This method encourages employees unity as employees of a particular group/cadre get equal salaries.

   There are some drawbacks of Time Rate Method, such as, it leads to tight supervision, indefinite employee cost, lesser efficiency of employees as there is no distinction made between efficient and inefficient employees, and lesser morale of employees.

   Time rate system is more suitable where the work is non-repetitive in nature and emphasis is more on quality output rather than quantity output.

2. **Piece Rate Method:** It is a method of compensation in which remuneration is paid on the basis of units or pieces produced by an employee. In this system emphasis is more on quantity output rather than quality output. Under this system the determination of employee cost per unit is not difficult because salaries differ with output. There is less supervision required under this method and hence the per unit cost of production is low. This system improves the morale of the employees as the salaries are directly related with their work efforts. There is greater work-efficiency in this method.

There are some drawbacks of this method, such as, it is not easily computable, leads to deterioration in work quality, wastage of resources, lesser unity of employees, higher cost of production and insecurity among the employees.

Piece rate system is more suitable where the nature of work is repetitive and quantity is emphasized more than quality.

Directing Function of Management

DIRECTING is said to be a process in which the managers instruct, guide and oversee the performance of the workers to achieve predetermined goals. Directing is said to be the heart of management process. <u>Planning</u>, <u>organizing</u>, staffing have got no importance if direction function does not take place.

Directing initiates action and it is from here actual work starts. Direction is said to be consisting of human factors. In simple words, it can be described as providing guidance to workers is doing work. In field of management, direction is said to be all those activities which are designed to encourage the subordinates to work effectively and efficiently. According to Human, "Directing consists of process or technique by which instruction can be issued and operations can be carried out as originally planned" Therefore, Directing is the function of guiding, inspiring, overseeing and instructing people towards accomplishment of organizational goals.

Direction has got following characteristics:

1. **Pervasive Function** - Directing is required at all levels of organization. Every manager provides guidance and inspiration to his subordinates.
2. **Continuous Activity** - Direction is a continuous activity as it continuous throughout the life of organization.

3. **Human Factor** - Directing function is related to subordinates and therefore it is related to human factor. Since human factor is complex and behaviour is unpredictable, direction function becomes important.

4. **Creative Activity** - Direction function helps in converting plans into performance. Without this function, people become inactive and physical resources are meaningless.

5. **Executive Function** - Direction function is carried out by all managers and executives at all levels throughout the working of an enterprise, a subordinate receives instructions from his superior only.

6. **Delegate Function** - Direction is supposed to be a function dealing with human beings. Human behaviour is unpredictable by nature and conditioning the people's behaviour towards the goals of the enterprise is what the executive does in this function. Therefore, it is termed as having delicacy in it to tackle human behaviour.

Importance of Directing Function

Directing or Direction function is said to be the heart of management of process and therefore, is the central point around which accomplishment of goals take place. A few philosophers call Direction as *"Life spark of an enterprise"*. It is also called as on actuating function of management because it is through direction that the operation of an enterprise actually starts. Being the central character of enterprise, it provides many benefits to a concern which are as follows:-

1. **It Initiates Actions** - Directions is the function which is the starting point of the work performance of subordinates. It is from this function the action takes place, subordinates understand their jobs and do according to the instructions laid. Whatever are plans laid, can be implemented only once the actual work starts. It is there that direction becomes beneficial.

2. **It Ingrates Efforts** - Through direction, the superiors are able to guide, inspire and instruct the subordinates to work. For this, efforts of every individual towards accomplishment of goals are required. It is through direction the efforts of every department can be related and integrated with others. This can be done through persuasive leadership and effective communication. Integration of efforts bring effectiveness and stability in a concern.

3. **Means of Motivation** - Direction function helps in achievement of goals. A manager makes use of the element of motivation here to improve the performances of

subordinates. This can be done by providing incentives or compensation, whether monetary or non - monetary, which serves as a "Morale booster" to the subordinates Motivation is also helpful for the subordinates to give the best of their abilities which ultimately helps in growth.

4. **It Provides Stability -** Stability and balance in concern becomes very important for long term sun survival in the market. This can be brought upon by the managers with the help of four tools or elements of direction function - judicious blend of persuasive leadership, effective communication, strict supervision and efficient motivation. Stability is very important since that is an index of growth of an enterprise. Therefore a manager can use of all the four traits in him so that performance standards can be maintained.

5. **Coping up with the changes -** It is a human behaviour that human beings show resistance to change. Adaptability with changing environment helps in sustaining planned growth and becoming a market leader. It is directing function which is of use to meet with changes in environment, both internal as external. Effective communication helps in coping up with the changes. It is the role of manager here to communicate the nature and contents of changes very clearly

to the subordinates. This helps in clarifications, easy adaptions and smooth running of an enterprise. For example, if a concern shifts from handlooms to powerlooms, an important change in technique of production takes place. The resulting factors are less of manpower and more of machinery. This can be resisted by the subordinates. The manager here can explain that the change was in the benefit of the subordinates. Through more mechanization, production increases and thereby the profits. Indirectly, the subordinates are benefited out of that in form of higher remuneration.

6. **Efficient Utilization of Resources** - Direction finance helps in clarifying the role of every subordinate towards his work. The resources can be utilized properly only when less of wastages, duplication of efforts, overlapping of performances, etc. doesn't take place. Through direction, the role of subordinates become clear as manager makes use of his supervisory, the guidance, the instructions and motivation skill to inspire the subordinates. This helps in maximum possible utilization of resources of men, machine, materials and money which helps in reducing costs and increasing profits.

From the above discussion, one can justify that direction, surely, is the heart of management process. Heart plays an important role in a human body as it serves the function pumping blood to all parts of body which makes the parts function. In the similar manner, direction helps the subordinates to perform in best of their abilities and that too in a healthy environment. The manager makes use of the four elements of direction here so that work can be accomplished in a proper and right manner. According to Earnest Dale, "Directing is what has to be done and in what manner through dictating the procedures and policies for accomplishing performance standards". Therefore, it is rightly said that direction is essence of management process.

Role of a Supervisor

Supervisor has got an important role to play in factory management. Supervision means overseeing the subordinates at work at the factory level. The supervisor is a part of the management team and he holds the designation of first line managers. He is a person who has to perform many functions which helps in achieving productivity. Therefore, supervisor can be called as the only manager who has an important role at execution level. There are certain philosophers who call supervisors as workers. There are yet some more philosophers who call them as managers. But actually he should be called as a manager or operative manager. His primary job is to manage the workers at operative level of management.

A supervisor plays multiplinary role at one time like -

1. **As a Planner -** A supervisor has to plan the daily work schedules in the factory. At the same time he has to divide the work to various workers according to their abilities.

2. **As a Manager -** It is righty said that a supervisor is a part of the management team of an enterprise. He is, in fact, an operative manager.

3. **As a Guide and Leader -** A factory supervisor leads the workers by guiding them the way of perform their daily tasks. In fact, he plays a role of an inspirer by telling them.

4. **As a Mediator -** A Supervisor is called a linking pin between management and workers. He is the spokesperson of management as well as worker.

5. **As an Inspector -** An important role of supervisor is to enforce discipline in the factory. For this, the work includes checking progress of work against the time schedule, recording the work performances at regular intervals and reporting the deviations if any from those. He can also frame

rules and regulations which have to be followed by workers during their work.

6. **As a Counselor** - A supervisor plays the role of a counselor to the worker's problem. He has to perform this role in order to build good relations and co-operation from workers. This can be done not only by listening to the grievances but also handling the grievances and satisfying the workers.

Therefore, we can say that effective and efficient supervision helps in serving better work performance, building good human relations, creating a congenial and co-operative environment. This all helps in increasing productivity.

Functions of a Supervisor

Supervisor, being the manager in a direct contact with the operatives, has got multifarious function to perform. The objective behind performance of these functions is to bring stability and soundness in the organization which can be secured through increase in profits which is an end result of higher productivity. Therefore, a supervisor should be concerned with performing the following functions -

1. **Planning and Organizing** - Supervisor's basic role is to plan the daily work schedule of the workers by guiding them

the nature of their work and also dividing the work amongst the workers according to their interests, aptitudes, skills and interests.

2. **Provision of working conditions** - A supervisor plays an important role in the physical setting of the factory and in arranging the physical resources at right place. This involves providing proper sitting place, ventilation, lighting, water facilities etc. to workers. His main responsibility is here to provide healthy and hygienic condition to the workers.

3. **Leadership and Guidance** - A supervisor is the leader of workers under him. He leads the workers and influences them to work their best. He also guides the workers by fixing production targets and by providing them instruction and guidelines to achieve those targets.

4. **Motivation** - A supervisor plays an important role by providing different incentives to workers to perform better. There are different monetary and non-monetary incentives which can inspire the workers to work better.

5. **Controlling** - Controlling is an important function performed by supervisor. This will involve

    i. Recording the actual performance against the time schedule.

    ii. Checking of progress of work.

iii. Finding out deviations if any and making solutions

iv. If not independently solved, reporting it to top management.

6. **Linking Pin** - A supervisor proves to be a linking pin between management and workers. He communicates the policies of management to workers also passes instructions to them on behalf of management. On the other hand, he has a close contact with the workers and therefore can interact the problems, complaints, suggestions, etc to the management. In this way, he communicates workers problems and brings it to the notice of management.

7. **Grievance Handling** - The supervisor can handle the grievances of the workers effectively for this he has to do the following things :-

   i. He can be in direct touch with workers.

   ii. By winning the confidence of the workers by solving their problems.

   iii. By taking worker problems on humanitarian grounds.

   iv. If he cannot tackle it independently, he can take the help and advice of management to solve it.

8. **Reporting** - A supervisor has got an important role to report about the cost, quality and any such output which can be responsible for increasing productivity. Factors like cost,

output, performance, quality, etc can be reported continually to the management.

9. **Introducing new work methods** - The supervisor here has to be conscious about the environment of market and competition present. Therefore he can innovate the techniques of production. He can shift the workers into fresh schedules whenever possible. He can also try this best to keep on changing and improving to the physical environment around the workers. This will result in

    i.   Higher productivity,

    ii.   High Morale of Workers,

    iii.   Satisfying working condition,

    iv.   Improving human relations,

    v.   Higher Profits, and

    vi.   High Stability

10.   **Enforcing Discipline** - A supervisor can undertake many steps to maintain discipline in the concern by regulating checks and measures, strictness in orders and instructions, keeping an account of general discipline of factory, implementing penalties and punishments for the indiscipline workers. All these above steps help in improving the overall discipline of the factory.

Controlling Function of Management

What is Controlling?

Controlling consists of verifying whether everything occurs in confirmities with the plans adopted, instructions issued and principles established. Controlling ensures that there is effective and efficient utilization of organizational resources so as to achieve the planned goals. Controlling measures the deviation of actual performance from the standard performance, discovers the causes of such deviations and helps in taking corrective actions

According to Brech, "Controlling is a systematic exercise which is called as a process of checking actual performance against the standards or plans with a view to ensure adequate progress and also recording such experience as is gained as a contribution to possible future needs."

According to Donnell, "Just as a navigator continually takes reading to ensure whether he is relative to a planned action, so should a business manager continually take reading to assure himself that his enterprise is on right course."

Controlling has got two basic purposes

  1. It facilitates co-ordination

2. It helps in planning

Features of Controlling Function

Following are the characteristics of controlling function of management-

1. **Controlling is an end function-** A function which comes once the performances are made in confirmities with plans.

2. **Controlling is a pervasive function-** which means it is performed by managers at all levels and in all type of concerns.

3. **Controlling is forward looking-** because effective control is not possible without past being controlled. Controlling always look to future so that follow-up can be made whenever required.

4. **Controlling is a dynamic process-** since controlling requires taking reviewal methods, changes have to be made wherever possible.

5. **Controlling is related with planning-** Planning and Controlling are two inseperable functions of management. Without planning, controlling is a meaningless exercise and without controlling, planning is useless. *Planning presupposes controlling and controlling succeeds planning.*

Process of Controlling

Controlling as a management function involves following steps:

1. **Establishment of standards-** Standards are the plans or the targets which have to be achieved in the course of business function. They can also be called as the criterions for judging the performance. Standards generally are classified into two-

    a. Measurable or tangible - Those standards which can be measured and expressed are called as measurable standards. They can be in form of cost, output, expenditure, time, profit, etc.

    b. Non-measurable or intangible- There are standards which cannot be measured monetarily. For example- performance of a manager, deviation of workers, their attitudes towards a concern. These are called as intangible standards.

    Controlling becomes easy through establishment of these standards because controlling is exercised on the basis of these standards.

2. **Measurement of performance-** The second major step in controlling is to measure the performance. Finding out

deviations becomes easy through measuring the actual performance. Performance levels are sometimes easy to measure and sometimes difficult. Measurement of tangible standards is easy as it can be expressed in units, cost, money terms, etc. Quantitative measurement becomes difficult when performance of manager has to be measured. Performance of a manager cannot be measured in quantities. It can be measured only by-

    a. Attitude of the workers,

    b. Their morale to work,

    c. The development in the attitudes regarding the physical environment, and

    d. Their communication with the superiors.

It is also sometimes done through various reports like weekly, monthly, quarterly, yearly reports.

3. **Comparison of actual and standard performance-** Comparison of actual performance with the planned targets is very important. Deviation can be defined as the gap between actual performance and the planned targets. The manager has to find out two things here- extent of deviation and cause of deviation. Extent of deviation means that the manager has to find out whether the deviation is positive or

negative or whether the actual performance is in conformity with the planned performance. The managers have to exercise control by exception. He has to find out those deviations which are critical and important for business. Minor deviations have to be ignored. Major deviations like replacement of machinery, appointment of workers, quality of raw material, rate of profits, etc. should be looked upon consciously. Therefore it is said, " If a manager controls everything, he ends up controlling nothing." For example, if stationery charges increase by a minor 5 to 10%, it can be called as a minor deviation. On the other hand, if monthly production decreases continuously, it is called as major deviation.

Once the deviation is identified, a manager has to think about various cause which has led to deviation. The causes can be-

    a. Erroneous planning,
    b. Co-ordination loosens,
    c. Implementation of plans is defective, and
    d. Supervision and communication is ineffective, etc.

4. **Taking remedial actions**- Once the causes and extent of deviations are known, the manager has to detect those errors

and take remedial measures for it. There are two alternatives here-

a. Taking corrective measures for deviations which have occurred; and

b. After taking the corrective measures, if the actual performance is not in conformity with plans, the manager can revise the targets. It is here the controlling process comes to an end. Follow up is an important step because it is only through taking corrective measures, a manager can exercise controlling.

Relationship between planning and controlling

Planning and controlling are two separate fuctions of management, yet they are closely related. The scope of activities if both are overlapping to each other. Without the basis of planning, controlling activities becomes baseless and without controlling, planning becomes a meaningless exercise. In absense of controlling, no purpose can be served by. Therefore, planning and controlling reinforce each other. According to Billy Goetz, " Relationship between the two can be summarized in the following points

Planning preceeds controlling and controlling succeeds planning.

Planning and controlling are inseperable functions of management.

Activities are put on rails by planning and they are kept at right place through controlling.

The process of planning and controlling works on Systems Approach which is as follows :

Planning $\rightarrow$ Results $\rightarrow$ Corrective Action

Planning and controlling are integral parts of an organization as both are important for smooth running of an enterprise.

Planning and controlling reinforce each other. Each drives the other function of management.

In the present dynamic environment which affects the organization, the strong relationship between the two is very critical and important. In the present day environment, it is quite likely that planning fails due to some unforeseen events. There controlling comes to the rescue. Once controlling is done effectively, it give us stimulus to make better plans. Therfore, planning and controlling are inseperate functions of a business enterprise.

Meaning of Controlling

Controlling is one of the important functions of a manager. In order to seek planned results from the subordinates, a manager needs to exercise effective control over the activities of the subordinates. In other words, controlling means ensuring that activities in an organisation are performed as per the plans. Controlling also ensures that an organisation's resources are being used effectively and efficiently for the achievement of predetermined goals. Controlling is, thus, a goal-oriented function.

Controlling function of a manager is a pervasive function. It is a primary function of every manager. Managers at all levels of management- top, middle and lower-need to perform controlling functions to keep a control over activities in their areas. Moreover, controlling is as much required in an educational institution, military, hospital, and a club as in any business organisation.

Controlling should not be misunderstood as the last function of management. It is a function that brings back the management cycle back to the planning function. The controlling function finds out how far actual performance deviates from standards, analyses the causes of such deviations and attempts to take corrective actions based on the same. This process helps in formulation of future plans in the light of the problems that were identified and, thus, helps in better planning in the future periods. Thus, controlling only completes one cycle of management process and improves planning in the next cycle.

Importance of Controlling

Control is an indispensable function of management. Without control the best of plans can go awry. A good control system helps an organisation in the following ways:

(i) **Accomplishing organisational goals:** The controlling function measures progress towards the organisational goals and brings to light the deviations, if any, and indicates corrective action. It, thus, guides the organisation and keeps it on the right track so that organisational goals might be achieved.

(ii) **Judging accuracy of standards:** A good control system enables management to verify whether the standards set are accurate and objective. An efficient control system keeps a careful check on the changes taking place in the organisation and in the environment and helps to review and revise the standards in light of such changes.

(iii) **Making efficient use of resources:** By exercising control, a manager seeks to reduce wastage and spoilage of resources. Each activity is performed in accordance with predetermined standards and norms. This ensures that resources are used in the most effective and efficient manner.

(iv) **Improving employee motivation:** A good control system ensures that employees know well in advance what they are expected to do and what are the standards of performance on the basis of which they will be appraised. It, thus, motivates them and helps them to give better performance.

(v) **Ensuring order and discipline:** Controlling creates an atmosphere of order and discipline in the organisation. It helps to minimise dishonest behaviour on the part of the employees by keeping a close check on their activities. The box explains how an import-export company was able to track dishonest employees by using computer monitoring as a part of their control system.

(vi) **Facilitating coordination in action:** Controlling provides direction to all activities and efforts for achieving organisational goals. Each department and employee is governed by predetermined standards which are well coordinated with one another. This ensures that overall organisational objectives are accomplished.

Limitations of Controlling

Although controlling is an important function of management, it suffers from the following limitations.

(i) **Difficulty in setting quantitative standards:** Control system loses some of its effectiveness when standards cannot be defined in quantitative terms. This makes measurement of performance and their comparison with standards a difficult task. Employee morale, job satisfaction and human behaviour are such areas where this problem might arise.

(ii) **Little control on external factors:** Generally an enterprise cannot control external factors such as government policies, technological changes, competition etc.

(iii) **Resistance from employees:** Control is often resisted by employees. They see it as a restriction on their freedom. For instance, employees might object when they are kept under a strict watch with the help of Closed Circuit Televisions (CCTVs).

Remain level headed even when things go wrong
Controlling

(iv) **Costly affair:** Control is a costly affair as it involves a lot of expenditure, time and effort. A small enterprise cannot afford to install an expensive control system. It cannot justify the expenses involved. Managers must ensure that the costs of installing and operating a control system should not exceed the benefits derived from it.

Relationship between Planning and Controlling

Planning and controlling are inseparable twins of management. A system of control presupposes the existence of certain standards. These standards of performance which serve as the basis of controlling are provided by planning. Once a plan becomes operational, controlling is necessary to monitor the progress, measure it, discover deviations and initiate corrective measures to ensure that events conform to plans. Thus, planning without controlling is meaningless. Similarly, controlling is blind without planning. If the standards are not set in advance, managers have nothing to control. When there is no plan, there is no basis of controlling.

Planning is clearly a prerequisite for controlling. It is utterly foolish to think that controlling could be accomplished without planning. Without planning there is no predetermined understanding of the desired performance. Planning seeks consistent, integrated and articulated programmes while controlling seeks to compel events to conform to plans.

Planning is basically an intellectual process involving thinking, articulation and analysis to discover and prescribe an appropriate course of action for achieving objectives. Controlling, on the other hand, checks whether decisions have been translated into desired action. Planning is thus, prescriptive whereas, controlling is evaluative.

It is often said that planning is looking ahead while controlling is looking back. However, the statement is only partially correct. Plans are prepared for future and are based on forecasts about future conditions. Therefore, planning involves looking ahead and is called a forward-looking function. On the contrary, controlling is like a postmortem of past activities to find out deviations from the standards. In that sense, controlling is a backward-looking function. However, it should be understood that planning is guided by past experiences and the corrective action initiated by control function aims to improve future performance. Thus, planning and controlling are both backward-looking as well as a forward-looking function.

Thus, planning and controlling are interrelated and, in fact, reinforce each other in the sense that 1. Planning based on facts makes controlling easier and effective; and

2. Controlling improves future planning by providing information derived from past experience.

Controlling Process

Controlling is a systematic process involving the following steps.

1. Setting performance standards

2. Measurement of actual performance

3. Comparison of actual performance with standards

4. Analysing deviations

5. Taking corrective action

Step 1: *Setting Performance Standards:* The first step in the controlling process is setting up of performance standards. Standards are the criteria against which actual performance would be measured. Thus, standards serve as benchmarks towards which an organisation strives to work.

Standards can be set in both quantitative as well as qualitative terms. For instance, standards set in terms of cost to be incurred, revenue to be earned, product units to be produced and sold, time to be spent in performing a task, all represents quantitative standards. Sometimes standards may also be set in qualitative terms. Improving goodwill and motivation level of employees are examples of qualitative standards. The table in the next page gives a glimpse of standards used in different functional areas of business to gauge performance.

At the time of setting standards, a manager should try to set standards in precise quantitative terms as this would make their comparison with actual performance much easier. For instance, reduction of defects from 10 in every 1,000 pieces produced to 5 in every 1,000 pieces produced by the end of the quarter.

However, whenever qualitative standards are set, an effort must be made to define them in a manner that would make their measurement easier. For instance, for improving customer satisfaction in a fast food chain having self-service, standards can be set in terms of time taken by a customer to wait for a table, time taken by him to place the order and time taken to collect the order.

It is important that standards should be flexible enough to be modified whenever required. Due to changes taking place in the internal and external business environment, standards may need some modification to be realistic in the changed business environment.

Step 2: *Measurement of Actual Performance:* Once performance standards are set, the next step is measurement of actual performance. Performance should be measured in an objective and reliable manner. There are several techniques for measurement of performance. These include personal observation, sample checking, performance reports, etc. As far as possible, performance should be measured in the same units in which standards are set as this would make their comparison easier.

It is generally believed that measurement should be done after the task is completed. However, wherever possible, measurement of work should be done during the performance. For instance, in case of assembling task, each part produced should be checked before assembling. Similarly, in a manufacturing plant, levels of gas particles in the air could be continuously monitored for safety.

Measurement of performance of an employee may require preparation of performance report by his superior. Measurement of a company's performance may involve calculation of certain ratios like gross profit ratio, net profit ratio, return on investment, etc., at periodic intervals. Progress of work in certain operating areas like marketing may be measured by considering the number of units sold, increase in market share etc., whereas, efficiency of production may be measured by counting the number of pieces produced and number of defective pieces in a batch. In small organisations, each piece produced may be checked to ensure that it conforms to quality specifications laid down for the product. However, this might not be possible in a large organisation. Thus, in large organisations, certain pieces are checked at random for quality. This is known as sample checking.

Step 3: *Comparing Actual Performance with Standards:* This step involves comparison of actual performance with the standard. Such comparison will reveal the deviation between actual and desired results. Comparison becomes easier when standards are set in quantitative terms. For instance, performance of a worker in terms of units produced in a week can be easily measured against the standard output for the week.

Step 4: *Analysing Deviations:* Some deviation in performance can be expected in all activities. It is, therefore, important to determine the acceptable range of deviations. Also, deviations in key areas of business need to be attended more urgently as compared to deviations in certain insignificant areas. Critical point control and management by exception should be used by a manager in this regard.

1. *Critical Point Control:* It is neither economical nor easy to keep a check on each and every activity in an organisation. Control should, therefore, focus on key result areas (KRAs) which are critical to the success of an organisation. These KRAs are set as the critical points. If anything goes wrong at the critical points, the entire organisation suffers. For instance, in a manufacturing organisation, an increase of 5 per cent in the labour cost may be more troublesome than a 15 per cent increase in postal charges.

2. *Management by Exception:* Management by exception, which is often referred to as control by exception, is an important principle of management control based on the belief that an attempt to control everything results in controlling nothing. Thus, only significant deviations which go beyond the

permissible limitshould be brought to the notice of management. Thus, if the plans lay down 2 per cent increase in labour cost as an acceptable range of deviation in a manufacturing organisation, only increase in labour cost beyond 2 per cent should be brought to the notice of the management. However, in case of major deviation from the standard (say, 5 per cent), the matter has to receive immediate action of management on a priority basis.

After identifying the deviations that demand managerial attention, these deviations need to be analysed for their causes. Deviations may have multiple causes for their origin. These include unrealistic standards, defective process, inadequacy of resources, structural drawbacks, organisational constraints and environmental factors beyond the control of the organisation. It is necessary to identify the exact cause(s) of deviations, failing which, an appropriate corrective action might not be possible. The deviations and their causes are then reported and corrective action taken at appropriate level.

Step 5: *Taking Corrective Action:* The final step in the controlling process is taking corrective action. No corrective action is required when the deviations are within acceptable limits. However, when the deviations go beyond the acceptable range, especially in the important areas, it demands immediate managerial attention so that deviations do not occur again and standards are accomplished.

Corrective action might involve training of employees if the production target could not be met. Similarly, if an important project is running behind schedule, corrective action might involve assigning of additional workers and equipment to the project and permission for overtime work.

Techniques of Managerial Control

The various techniques of managerial control may be classified into two broad categories: traditional techniques, and modern techniques.

Traditional Techniques

Traditional techniques are those which have been used by the companies for a long time now. However, these techniques have not become obsolete and are still being used by companies. These include: (a) Personal observation

(b) Statistical reports

(c) Breakeven analysis

(d) Budgetary control

Modern Techniques

Modern techniques of controlling are those which are of recent origin and are comparatively new in management literature.

These techniques provide a refreshingly new thinking on the ways in which various aspects of an organisation can be controlled. These include:

(a) Return on investment

(b) Ratio analysis

(c) Responsibility accounting

(d) Management audit

(e) PERT and CPM

(f) Management information system

Traditional Techniques

Personal Observation

This is the most traditional method of control. Personal observation enables the manager to collect first hand information. It also creates a psychological pressure on the employees to perform well as they are aware that they are being observed personally on their job. However, it is a very time-consuming exercise and cannot effectively be used in all kinds of jobs.

Statistical Reports

Statistical analysis in the form of averages, percentages, ratios, correlation, etc., present useful information to the managers regarding performance of the organisation in various areas. Such information when presented in the form of charts, graphs, tables, etc., enables the managers to read them more easily and allow a comparison to be made with performance in previous periods and also with the benchmarks.

Breakeven Analysis

Breakeven analysis is a technique used by managers to study the relationship between costs, volume and profits. It determines the probable profit and losses at different levels of activity. The sales volume at which Breakeven point can be calculated with the help of the following formula:

Breakeven Point = Fixed Costs

Selling price per unit – Variable cost per unit

Breakeven analysis helps a firm in keeping a close check over its variable costs and determines the level of activity at which the firm can earn its target profit.

Budgetary Control

Budgetary control is a technique of managerial control in which all operations are planned in advance in the form of budgets and actual results are compared with budgetary standards. This comparison reveals the necessary actions to be taken so that organisational objectives are accomplished.

A budget is a quantitative statement for a definite future period of time for the purpose of obtaining a given objective. It is also a statement which reflects the policy of that particular period. It will contain figures of forecasts both in terms of time and quantities. The box shows the most common types of budgets used by an organisation.

Budgeting offers the following advantages: 1. Budgeting focuses on specific and time-bound targets and thus, helps in attainment of organisational objectives.

2. Budgeting is a source of motivation to the employees who know the standards against which their performance will be appraised and thus, enables them to perform better.

3. Budgeting helps in optimum utilisation of resources by allocating them according to the requirements of different departments.

4. Budgeting is also used for achieving coordination among different departments of an organisation and highlights the interdependence between them. For instance, sales budget cannot be prepared without knowing production programmes and schedules.

5. It facilitates management by exception by stressing on those operations which deviate from budgeted standards in a significant way.

However, the effectiveness of budgeting depends on how accurately estimates have been made about future. Flexible budgets should be prepared which can be adopted if forecasts about future turn out to be different, especially in the face of changing environmental forces. Managers must remember that budgeting should not be viewed as an end but a means to achieve organisational objectives.

Modern Techniques

Return on Investment

Return on Investment (RoI) is a useful technique which provides the basic yardstick for measuring whether or not invested capital has been used effectively for generating reasonable amount of return. RoI can be used to measure overall performance of an organisation or of its individual departments or divisions. It can be calculated as under.

Net Income Sales

Net Income before or after tax may be used for making comparisons. Total investment includes both working as well as fixed capital invested in business. According to this technique, RoI can be increased either by increasing sales volume proportionately more than total investment or by reducing total investment without having any reductions in sales volume.

RoI provides top management an effective means of control for measuring and comparing performance of different departments.

It also permits departmental managers to find out the problem which affects RoI in an adverse manner.

Ratio Analysis

Ratio Analysis refers to analysis of financial statements through computation of ratios. The most commonly used ratios used by organisations can be classified into the following categories:

1. *Liquidity Ratios:* Liquidity ratios are calculated to determine short-term solvency of business. Analysis of current position of liquid funds determines the ability of the business to pay the amount due to its stakeholders.

2. *Solvency Ratios:* Ratios which are calculated to determine the long-term solvency of business are known as solvency ratios. Thus, these ratios determine the ability of a business to service its indebtedness.

3. *Profitability Ratios:* These ratios are calculated to analyse the profitability position of a business. Such ratios involve analysis of profits in relation to sales or funds or capital employed.

4. *Turnover Ratios:* Turnover ratios are calculated to determine the efficiency of operations based on effective utilisation of resources. Higher turnover means better utilisation of resources.

The table given below gives examples of some ratios commonly used by managers.

Examples of Commonly used Ratios

Type of Ratio	Examples
Liquidity	Current Ratio
	Quick Ratio
Solvency	Debt-Equity Ratio
	Proprietary Ratio
	Interest Coverage Ratio
Profitability	Gross Profit Ratio
	Net Profit Ratio
	Return on Capital Employed
Turnover	Inventory Turnover Ratio
	Stock Turn over Ratio
	Debtors Turn over Ratio

www.ingramcontent.com/pod-product-compliance
Lightning Source LLC
Chambersburg PA
CBHW080819180526
45168CB00006B/2506